Making
Memories

IDEAS FOR FAMILY MISSION INVOLVEMENT

Mary Ann Ward Appling

ABOUT THE WRITER

Mary Ann Ward Appling is a writer, wife, and mother of two living in Birmingham, Alabama.

New Hope

P. O. Box 12065

Birmingham, AL 35202-2065

Lenore Stringer, Contributing editor

Scripture quotations identified NIV are taken from the *Holy Bible: New International Version* © 1978 by the Internatinal Bible Society. Used by permission of Zondervan Bible Publishers.

Dewey Decimal Classification: 249

Subject Headings:

MISSIONS ACTIVITIES

FAMILY—RELIGIOUS LIFE

FAMILY LIFE

N934109•0793•5M1

ISBN: 1-56309-077-5

SPRING

SUMMER

FALL

WINTER

INTRODUCTION

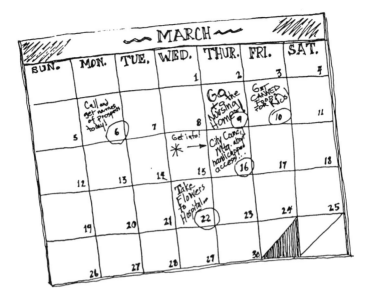

We may be anywhere when it happens—at the grocery store, riding in the car, or at home in the midst of work or play. In the middle of routine tasks, one of my children will punctuate our running dialogue with, "Momma, remember the time when . . . ?"

Because Elizabeth and Andrew are young, ages four and six, I did not expect them to share memories at this stage of life. I thought that would come much later. Yet, they began recalling memories almost as soon as they began talking in complete sentences. Not all of their early memories have stayed with them. But as some fade, others take their place.

As I've watched this interesting process develop, I've thought about the permanent memories they will carry into adulthood. Will they be memories that matter?

Memories are powerful links to the past that irrevocably influence the future. Good or bad, we all have them. They connect us to people and experiences and values that leave fingerprints on our lives.

I want my children to grow up with a rich heritage of memories of our family life. But I also want those memories to point them to a God-focused life-style so they can see their grown-up world through God's eyes and act accordingly. I want their lives to count for something eternal. My prayer is that they will have unswerving commitments to minister in Christ's name and make Him known.

How will this happen? Will memories from their childhoods motivate them or hinder them from growing up to become adults God can use to accomplish His purposes?

The jury is still out on that in our family. It will be years before we see measurable or permanent results from these years together. So, what can I do now to influence the outcome? What can you do if you want your children to have memories that matter in the eternal scheme of things?

You and I can build into our family lives experiences that produce meaningful missions memories. When I first became a parent, I began noticing the things we do with our children that are passed down from generation to generation. Many are empty in content and teaching value. One day, while doing "This Little Piggy Went to Market" on my baby's toes, I realized something. This activity had a high fun value, but I wondered why parents have passed on a little rhyme that is basically meaningless and nonsensical. Why did this last through the generations? I began wondering, what else could we do that was equally as fun but richer in meaning?

I learned something from this mental exercise. If we're not careful, we can load our children's memories with things that are fun and have pleasant associations but are empty. Perhaps we do this because it requires no advance planning or thought. We repeat what we've heard elsewhere in order to capture the moment. That certainly has its place in the ebb and flow of family life. Wouldn't family life, and memories, be richer if the activities and events captured in memory were planned for a purpose and designed to teach the truths of God's plan for His people and His world?

This book takes you through the seasons of the year. Obviously, you will have to adapt activities according to the ages of your children, their interests, and your circumstances. Use this as an idea book to make memories that matter as you raise children with a heart for missions. Realize that time spent now may yield eternal dividends.

 # SPRING

In my parents' backyard stands a large oak tree, somewhat unusual for their location in Texas. It's a focal point in their yard and a definite conversation piece. But our family remembers when that tree wasn't there.

It grew from an acorn that my mother picked up at a friend's house. She tossed the seed into a flower bed outside the back door, just to see what would happen. Soon, a small, tender plant sprouted. Then it grew so big it needed to be transplanted. That's when it found a home in the middle of our backyard. Through the years, we were not consciously aware of its steady growth, but it stands strong today, a product of a seed that sprouted one spring long ago.

Spring is also a time for planting spiritual seeds—seeds that produce memories of activities and relationships that advance God's purposes. Each seed that sprouts sends up a visible stem and emerging foliage. But beneath the surface, a root system also develops. The roots support the plant and receive nutrients from the soil. No one sees the roots do their work, but they are essential to the plant's well-being.

This spring, look for ways to plant seeds that contribute to missions memories in your family. Acts of kindness toward other people as you and your children minister in Jesus' name, feed the root system that they'll need to grow into adults who function as Great Commission Christians.

"But the fruit of the Spirit is love, joy, peace, patience, kindness, goodness, faithfulness, gentleness and self-control."

(Gal. 5:22-23 NIV)

PLAN, PLANT, AND POT

Spring is the time to polish your gardening skills and find the peat pots, hoe, and other trademarks of the green-thumb gang. This year your motives for planting may be a bit different from other years. This year you will be planting and potting with missions in mind!

When the fruits of your planning, planting, and potting come to full flower, you will be ready to share some of the beauty of the season with some people who need to be reminded that spring has come and there is reason for renewed hope and renewed purpose. Think about some of the people you know who need to see you and your family coming up to their door, carrying a room-brightening gift from your window garden or yard.

As you plant seeds and pot bulbs, explain to the children that God planned for people to take care of His world and enjoy the beauty that He makes possible. Tell the children that some of the plants will be used to cheer up people who have been homebound or lonely during the winter months.

Explain in simple terms that when we plant, God makes things grow. Also make it clear to the younger children that it will take several days before they see the plants peeping up through the soil, and it will take even longer before the plants will be ready to share with others. If you wish, assign a routine watering schedule for older children.

Occasionally during the growing cycle, remind the children that the plants have a special purpose. As you talk about and care for the plants, say things such as: "This plant may be the one we give to Mrs. Adams. I hope that she is feeling well today. We can ask God to help her today. We can call her on the phone sometime soon. We will not tell her about this plant. It will be our surprise."

SING ABOUT MISSIONS

Use music to create an awareness of the importance of Christian missions. With younger children sing songs such as "Jesus Loves the Little Children of the World." Make a brief comment that God sent His Son, Jesus, because He loves all the children of the world. With older children sing this song, substituting names of various countries of the world.

If you have an Autoharp or a piano, you may teach children this song with a foreign missions flavor. Ask the children to think about ways your church helps boys and girls of other lands learn that Jesus loves them.

Learn of God's Love

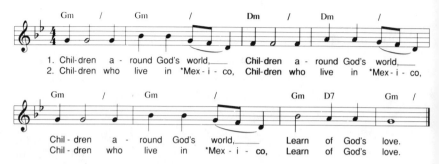

1. Chil-dren a - round God's world,___ Chil-dren a - round God's world,___
2. Chil-dren who live in *Mex - i - co, Chil-dren who live in *Mex - i - co,

Chil - dren a - round God's world,___ Learn of God's love.
Chil - dren who live in *Mex - i - co, Learn of God's love.

*Substitute names of other countries.

Words by DAVID ROSEMONT, adapted by Nan Grantham. Music American Folk **Melody**. **Words** © copyright 1982 Broadman Press (SESAC). All rights reserved. International copyright secured. Used by permission.

Children of Other Lands

1. In oth - er lands a - cross the sea, Are
2. In coun - tries near, and coun - tries far, Wher -

man - y chil - dren just like me:___ And
ev - er lit - tle chil - dren are,___ We

I must help to tell them there, That__
need to make them un - der - stand That__

Je - sus' love is ev - 'ry - where. } For
He loves those of ev - 'ry land. }

Je - sus loves the chil - dren A - cross the

wa - ters blue. If they do not know, we must

tell them so; Then they will love Him, too.

7

Words and music by ALAN GRAY M. CAMPBELL.

PLAY MUSICAL INSTRUMENTS

Scout around your kitchen, garage, and attic for some items that can be used as primitive musical instruments, such as shakers, drums, cymbals, and chimes. Tell the children that missionaries in different countries use music to teach people about Jesus. The missionaries encourage the people to play their own musical instruments as they sing new songs about Jesus. Sometimes the people sing the same songs that we sing in our churches, but the words are in another language.

Give your children some "instruments" that you have gathered. Provide wooden or plastic spoons to use as drumsticks, scratchers, and strikers. Sing a children's song, such as "Jesus Loves Me," and show the children how to beat rhythm as you sing together.

If the children are older, they may enjoy singing "Jesus Loves Me" in another language. The following words are that song in two other languages.

Christo Me Ama
(Jesus Loves Me)

The following song is the Spanish version of the same song.

Wa Ga Shu Esu
(Jesus Loves Me)

The following song is the Japanese version of the same song.

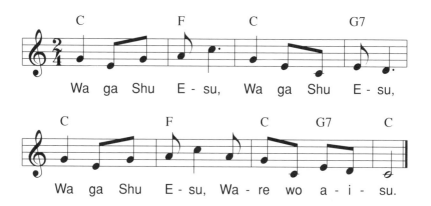

Wa ga Shu E - su, Wa ga Shu E - su,

Wa ga Shu E - su, Wa - re wo a - i - su.

English words by ANNA B. WARNER. Japanese translation unknown. Music by WILLIAM B. BRADBURY.

OBSERVE A PASSOVER FEAST

As the Easter season nears, find out where a Christian observance of the Passover will be held. Find out whether there will be a charge for the meal or some other plan, such as a covered-dish supper. Find out how and when to make reservations.

Before the event, prepare your children by explaining the biblical significance of the Passover. Explain that Jesus ate the Passover meal with His friends on the night He was arrested, tried, and crucified the next day. Explain that even today Jewish people keep the feast each year as they celebrate God's goodness to them when Moses and the Hebrew people were delivered from slavery in Egypt. Further explain that the Christian observance of the Passover can help your family understand more about how to be ministers to Jewish people.

SPRING BASKET OF GOODIES

Most people like baskets. A popular item for spring is a frilly basket filled with homemade goodies, neat trial-size cosmetic and toiletry items. Of course, if the person you have in mind is not the frilly-basket type, there are all kinds of containers in the hardware store that will appeal to men and boys on your list.

Lead the children to think about what they would like to put into a basket or baskets to give to persons who need a special lift during this spring season. Consider persons who have experienced illness, loneliness, bereavement, or traumatic change. If necessary, narrow your list so that you can arrange at least one ample basket that you can present.

Include the children in the planning, shopping, arranging, and delivery. Set a time to deliver the gift when the children can go with you. Call the person to whom you will give the basket and ask when it will be convenient for you and the children to drop by. Remind the children that you planned this gift to let the person who receives it know that he or she is loved.

SPRING MISSIONS OFFERING

Many churches have a special missions offering each spring. Find out what the missions offering is called in your church. Some Methodist churches sponsor a special missions offering called "Parable of Talents." Some Baptist churches have an offering called Annie Armstrong Easter Offering for Home Missions. Find out whether your church participates in missions offerings such as these. Make plans for how your family can participate in giving to the spring missions offering at your church.

Here are some suggestions for helping your children learn about the importance of working together with other Christians to support missions work here at home as well as around the world.

- Make a special bank in which the entire family can collect the money which will eventually be placed in a special offering envelope.
- Participate in your church's missions education opportunities that are associated with the time of the spring missions offering in your church.
- Find out how the missions offering will be used and tell your children about the plans for the offering.
- Find out why and when the offering was begun. Tell the children a brief history of the offering.
- Attend church worship service together and place the family's offering in the collection plate.
- Secure names of missionaries and pray for them, including the children in the brief prayertime.

MAKE EASTER CARDS

The Christian celebration of the resurrection sometimes is overshadowed by the commercial side of the season. If in your shopping you do not find greeting cards that reflect your Christian joy in this season, set out to make your own cards. Give attention to the design of the postage stamps you will use, choosing some that will convey the idea of spring.

Make a list of names and current addresses of people to whom the cards will be sent. Remember military personnel, the homebound, older relatives, missionaries whom you know personally, your minister, and others for whom your cards will have special meaning.

Encourage the children to make cards or sign the purchased cards that you will send. Lead them to recall favorite Bible verses that would be appropriate to write on one panel of the homemade cards.

As you work on making, signing, and addressing the cards, talk with the children about the Christian meaning of the Easter season. Be sure to stress the fact that the best news the world has ever heard is that Jesus arose from the dead and that He is alive. At some point in the process, pray a brief conversational prayer, thanking God that He sent His Son to be the Saviour of the world.

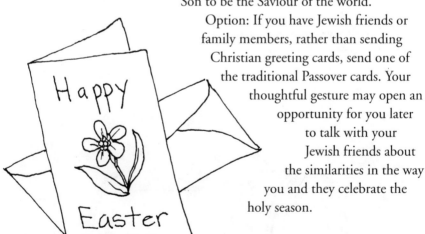

Option: If you have Jewish friends or family members, rather than sending Christian greeting cards, send one of the traditional Passover cards. Your thoughtful gesture may open an opportunity for you later to talk with your Jewish friends about the similarities in the way you and they celebrate the holy season.

STOCK, THEN RAID YOUR PANTRY

Each spring many communities advertise the need for food items to replenish help centers. The food drives are known by various names, but they have the same purpose. Decide now to be ready when you hear the plea for food for the needy.

Think about non-perishable items to include in your grocery purchases each time you do major shopping. Stock a separate shelf in your pantry or reserve the items in a special box or bag and resolve not to invade that stash until you have what you intend to donate to the food drive.

Tell the children what the extra food is for. Occasionally during mealtime prayer, pray for the homeless and for people in your town who do not have enough to eat. Encourage your children to be generous in sharing with the needy around them.

INTERNATIONAL MEAL

It is becoming a familiar experience to see persons from the distant corners of the world right next to us at the produce counter at the grocery. It is not unusual in some cities and towns in the United States to hear several languages spoken while shopping. Truly, missions opportunities have come to our door!

Make opportunities to meet and become better acquainted with internationals in your community. Talk with your children about the importance of respecting persons who are of different races and nationalities.

Consider the possibility of working with another family from your church who has children to arrange a social gathering to honor one or two international families who have recently moved to your community. Your guests probably will be more comfortable if they know one another and speak the same language.

After you make preliminary arrangements and invite the guests, confirm the invitations in writing, giving detailed directions to your home, the date, and the time. Then plan an all-American meal, including some food items that the internationals should recognize and enjoy.

Encourage the children to be part of the planning and preparations. Guide the children to plan recreation for the international children.

Option: If your home is not adequate for such a social gathering, consider enlisting the help of an adult group in your church. Have the meal in a designated area of your church building. With this plan, additional international guests can be invited. Regardless of which plan you choose, be prepared to converse with the guests and help them understand more about American customs related to home, church, and community.

SPRING CLEAR YOUR CLOSETS

There is a difference between spring cleaning your closets and spring clearing your closets. The latter can have a missions purpose.

At help centers in many cities, the workers are braced for a deluge of stuff that will come to them as a result of spring cleaning. You, too, may have witnessed the useless or badly worn items that are sometimes given in the name of charity. Resolve not to be guilty of giving dirty, badly worn items that will add to the pain and suffering already experienced by people needing to clothe themselves and their children.

As you clear closets of outgrown and off-season items which you can spare, stack them neatly and put them into containers so that they will not become soiled or wrinkled while they are being processed at the help centers. If possible, attach sizing tags to any garments that have lost the original size tags.

Explain to the children that this is a good way to give people a bit of extra help in clothing their families. Stress that Jesus told His followers to feed the hungry, visit the lonely, and clothe those who needed clothing.

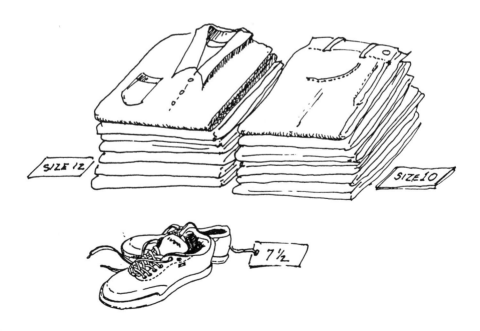

SLOW COOKER TO THE RESCUE

Keep your ears and eyes open for announcements about elderly persons in your church or community who have been ill or otherwise incapacitated recently. Some elderly persons neglect their nutrition when their routine is interrupted by adverse conditions. Shine up the slow cooker and get out your recipe books. Look for a dish that is suitable to take to an elderly person who may not have much appetite, but who desperately needs to eat well.

Inform your family of your plans and ask for other suggestions from them. Perhaps the children would like to make dessert suggestions. Plan to take the food in a disposable container which does not need to be returned to you.

Phone at least a day ahead of the planned delivery of the food so that the person will know that you are coming. In some cases it may be wise to remind the elderly person shortly before you are expected to arrive. If you think it appropriate, take your children with you as you deliver the food. On the way to the home, discuss with the children some things they may want to say to the elderly person.

During the brief visit, the person may appreciate it if you prayed with him or her. Comfort the person appropriately. Report special needs to your pastor or an advocate for the elderly.

HALL OF FAME

Get copies of outdated missions newsletters and periodicals which contain pictures and stories about missionaries in the United States and in foreign countries. Gather some art paper, scissors, glue, and clear adhesive tape.

With the children, look through the pictures and selected stories and choose pictures to clip out and mount on art paper. Lead the children to decide what captions to write on the lower margins of the mounting paper. Let the children decide where in your home to display the missionary hall of fame. Leave the display up for several days and refer to it occasionally.

BIBLES TO GIVE

Shop for Bibles to give to people who do not have any. Check bookstore sale tables and your own supply for Bibles that are good enough to give.

Order a free catalog of Bibles, Scripture portions, and other Bible-related materials from American Bible Society, 1865 Broadway, New York, NY 10023. You will be pleased to learn that at such economical prices you can purchase several Bibles at one time.

Find out from your church leaders whether there is a local need for extra Bibles. For instance, perhaps prisoners in local law enforcement facilities would like to have Bibles of their own. Or perhaps your church has a language ministry or rescue ministry to persons who have recently arrived in the United States. Perhaps your children have noticed that some children who attend your church do not have Bibles of their own. If someone from your church is planning a volunteer missions trip, perhaps they would welcome some Bibles to take with them to give.

If you are in contact with missionaries who are currently serving in a foreign country, perhaps they would like for you to send a few copies of the Bible in the language spoken where they serve.

When the Bibles have been collected, be sure that nothing personal has been left in them. Then lead the entire family to think about the blessing the Bibles can be to those who receive them. Pray that the Bibles will go from your home to accomplish what God would have them accomplish.

A NEW WAY TO DO ZOO

As soon as it is warm enough to venture out to the zoo, plan to take the children to see the animals and other exhibits at your nearest zoo. As you tell the children about the treat that awaits them, also tell them that this is a chance to see certain kinds of animals that missionaries might see every day in the lands where they live and work.

As you drive to the zoo, create anticipation and help the children begin to think about what they are going to do at the zoo. For instance, say things such as: "I'm thinking of an animal with black and white stripes. What is the name of that animal?" If the children do not know that you are referring to a zebra, teach them to say the word. Continue with clues about some other animals that you are almost certain to find in the zoo which you will visit.

When you arrive at the zoo, keep the children near you so that you can both protect them and talk with them. Read the information on the cages, pens, and displays. Summarize the information for the children, telling only the main facts about the creatures. Be sure to tell the children what countries particular animals are from. If you know names of missionaries of the past or present who have worked in a certain country, say: "Our missionary (name) probably sees this animal living free in the country where (he/she) works. Wouldn't it be fun to watch these animals in their natural homes?"

SELECT EXOTIC FRUIT

At the food market, visit the produce department and look for fruit imported from other countries. Purchase at least one of several kinds of fruit that you do not ordinarily serve.

If you are not sure about some of the facts about the fruit, look up information in a dictionary or cookbook. Prepare the fruit and place small pieces of each variety on a separate dish for each child. Provide toothpicks for the children to use in the tasting and telling experience.

As you eat the fruit, lead the children to learn the names of the fruit and the countries from which they came. Say: "Missionaries who live in the countries where these things grow probably eat some of these same delicious foods every day. They may not have fast-food places like we have, but we don't have trees that grow things like this."

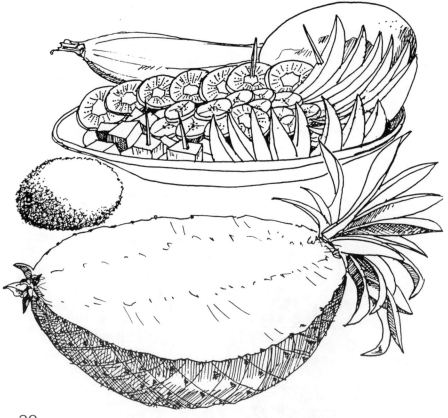

READING FUN FOR A RAINY DAY

Spring is almost certain to have its rainy days. When the children cannot go out to play, they look for things to do. Try reading a missionary biography written especially for children. Check the media library in your church or a Christian bookstore for a series of colorful, appealing missionary biographies which are appropriate for children in elementary grades. One series which is widely available is called "Meet the Missionary Series." The series contains 17 titles, each illustrated to accurately depict missions scenes. Five of the books in the series are also suitable to be read to older preschoolers.

Whatever selection you make, use this reading experience to let the children know that missionaries are real people with real families who have chosen to tell the good news about Jesus to people in other countries. If the children like to make up plays, guide them to make up a play based on an incident they heard in the book you read to them.

ATTEND A SUNRISE SERVICE

Churches in many communities cooperate in arranging and conducting Easter sunrise services. Find out about plans in your area for such an event.

Plan to give the children a light snack and bundle them up against the early morning chill. On the way to the service explain that a sunrise service helps us to remember that early on a Sunday morning, long, long ago, some women went to the place where Jesus had been buried. When they arrived at the burial place, the women found that Jesus had arisen from the dead. The women were the first people who got to tell the good news that Jesus was alive. Now we have the responsibility of telling the good news, too.

During the service, encourage the children to participate appropriately. Follow the outing with a real breakfast before going to your regular church service. If possible, treat the whole family to breakfast at a family-style restaurant. During the breakfast, talk about some aspects of the sunrise service and further explain anything the children did not fully understand.

NEIGHBORHOOD BLOCK PARTY

When the daylight hours become longer and the weather is warmer, ask some of the neighborhood parents whether they would like to sponsor a "get reacquainted" block party. Plan where, when, how long, and what style the party will take. Decide what lawn games to provide. Decide whether to put out lawn chairs. Keep refreshments simple because the real emphasis should be upon spending the time together playing games and talking.

If you have new neighbors, be sure they are invited to come and meet people who live around them. Have name tags ready for people to write on and pin on themselves.

After the initial get-acquainted time, you may have other opportunities to inquire about the church preference of some of your neighbors and invite them to be your guests at special events at your church. If some of the families will permit you to do so, you may arrange to transport their children to your church for summer events planned especially for children.

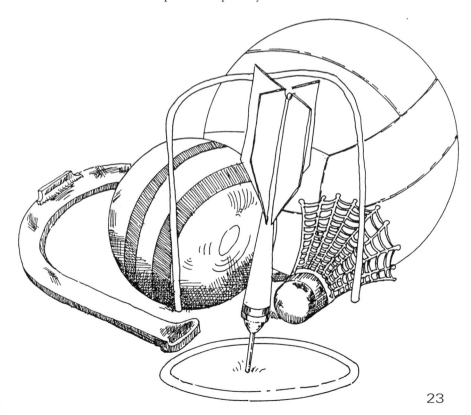

TALK LIKE THE MISSIONARIES TALK

Lead the children to develop an appreciation for the fact that English-speaking missionaries who go to foreign countries to tell about Jesus must learn the language of the people with whom they will be working. Think back to the days when you learned a foreign language in high school or in college. Use this guide to help you polish your accent before you teach this traditional question to the children.

Explain that there are several thousand American missionaries now working in many foreign countries, telling people about Jesus. Probably one of the questions the missionaries asked most frequently when they first arrived in the place where they would work was, "Do you speak English?" Many times no one else speaks English, and the missionary family must speak entirely in a foreign language. Lead the children to experience what it is like to learn and speak a foreign language as they learn *Do you speak English?*

Italian: Parla ingles?
[PAHR-lah een-GLEH-seh?]

German: Sprechen Sie Englisch?
[SHPREHKH-en zee ENG-lish?]

French: Parlez-vous l'anglais?
[Pahr-lay-voo lahn-gleh?]

Spanish: ?Hable usted ingles?
[Ahblah oostaydh eenglayss?]

RELATE YOUR
CONVERSION EXPERIENCE

Children need to realize that every person, including parents, have been invited by God's Word to believe in Jesus as Saviour and follow Him as Lord. You can help your children understand the Christian roots of your family by telling about your own Christian journey.

Tell about your first memory of going to church and what you remember learning. Tell about some of the Sunday School teachers you had or some of the people at church who made positive impressions on you.

Relate to the children who helped you know how to become a Christian and what they told you to do in order to become a Christian. If you attended a class for training new converts, tell what it was like. If you were given a presentation Bible or a certificate of baptism, show it to the children. Tell what it was like to be baptized.

Tell what you thought and felt about becoming a Christian. If you were young and felt timid about telling anyone that you wanted to learn more about becoming a Christian, tell your children. Perhaps they may be feeling some of those same kinds of uncertain feelings. Assure them that it is always acceptable to ask questions and to want to find out what it means to be a Christian.

As your children approach the time when they are ready to express their own faith in Jesus as Saviour, be ready to use Scripture passages, such as John 3:16; Romans 3:23; 5:8; 6:23; Acts 3:19; Ephesians 2:8; and Romans 10:13.

TELL A BIBLE MISSIONARY STORY

Children need to understand the relationship between the Great Commission Jesus gave to His followers and the present-day missions effort in the United States as well as in foreign countries. Explain that people in New Testament times carried out Jesus' order to go to all the world and tell the good news. Prepare to read or tell a Bible story about Paul, Philip, or one of your favorite missionaries of New Testament times.

If you don't have access to a Bible storybook for children, study one of the following Scripture passages and tell the story in an interesting storytelling style.

Philip and the man from Africa—Acts 8:26-40
Cornelius Calls for Peter—Acts 10
Barnabas and Saul Sent—Acts 13:1-34
Lydia Learns About Jesus—Acts 16:11-15
Paul, Prisoner and Missionary—Acts 28:17-31

If you have access to an illustrated Bible or an illustrated Bible storybook written especially for children, show the pictures as you read. Read one story at a sitting, taking into account that children need to talk about the story or debrief it in some manner. Perhaps they would like to tell the story or even decide on how to dramatize the story. Stay with the children, listen, and watch as they tell or dramatize the story.

At another time, choose another story and repeat the process. Think about other ways to vary the style in which you tell the story. Consider telling the story from a first person point of view. That is, you pretend to be the main character in the story.

SUMMER

You have almost 100 days of summer. But with the school year marching into June and sneaking up in August, summer seems to get shorter every year.

Summer can be a blip on the screen, or it can seem to last forever. If you are like most people, you probably start June with grand plans for things you would like to do with your family. But schedules overlap, money may be stretched, and crowds and weather can discourage you. If you are not careful, summer can come and go with lots of plans waiting to unfold and opportunities undiscovered.

Have you ever reached the end of summer and thought, "What did we do? Where did the time go?" Some people reach the empty nest years and wonder those same things. They remember what they wish they had done with their children instead of good times spent together.

Are there things you can do as a family this summer that will build memories and communicate the love of Jesus Christ as part of your family life-style?

Many things don't happen unless they are planned. That is true for vacation trips, special events, and family activities through which you reach out to others. Some things, once planned and implemented, become a part of your family life-style and memory bank. Once you have done them once or twice, they become habits or traditions.

I know several families who take an annual summer trip to a Christian conference center. This is not simply a pleasure trip; they conduct Bible school for Chinese children whose parents attend a Bible conference. One Anglo mom who helps every year told me that her family makes this a tradition so her children can interact with children whose cultural background is different than theirs.

This summer, plan some activities to help build missions memories for your family.

"A new command I give you: Love one another. . .
By this all men will know that you are my disciples,
if you love one another."

(John 13:34-35 NIV)

MISSIONS VACATION MAP

As you plan your next family vacation, get a map of the area you plan to visit. Place the map on the wall at the children's eye level. As you plan for the trip, talk about points of interest you will see on the trip. Take into account any historical mission sites or events significant in missions history.

If you are not aware of facts such as this, you may consult resources in your church media library or ask for help from your pastor. If you wish, you may order from the Chamber of Commerce or a travel agency serving the area you will visit, travel brochures or a directory of places which are significant in the development of Christian missions in the United States. An example of such a resource is *A Baptist Journey* by Tony Coursey, published by New Hope.

Seeing the places where historical missions events took place will bring a sense of reality to missions. Sights and sounds of real places will help make pioneer missionaries become more relevant to families of today.

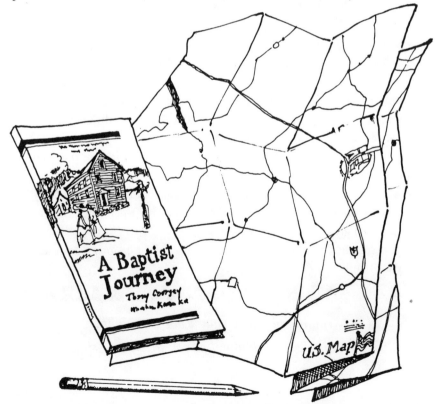

HELPFUL FAVORS FOR NURSING HOME RESIDENTS

In a nursing home or retirement center near you, there may be someone who is wishing for some ordinary service which will make a big difference in his or her life. With a suggestion from the social services office of the institution, you and your children can perform one or more of these favors.

• Perhaps you and your children can make, address, and mail greeting cards to family members for the resident.

• Perhaps you can read aloud to a resident who misses reading for himself because of declining vision.

• Offer to help the resident label clothing and personal articles.

• Enable the person to retain memory of names and places by assisting him in labeling photographs with names, places, and dates.

• Take the resident on an outing to visit a mall and make a purchase.

• Keep the resident informed about what is happening at his church by taking him bulletins and other information which he does not get in the mail.

• If the resident is mobile, invite him to accompany your family to a summer concert in the park.

• Offer to bring magazines and other reading material from your home or offer to bring cassette tapes or videotapes from your church media library or public library.

• During the summer take cut flowers on several of your visits and drop them off in the rooms of residents who are having a period of loneliness.

BRIGHTEN THE DAYS OF SICK CHILDREN

Find out what kinds of services or items are needed in the children's ward of a local health-care facility. If the hospital attracts patients from distant places, perhaps there will be parents and other caregivers who must stay in local motels or special housing provided by the hospital or agencies. Your comfort and thoughtfulness can be extended to this group, also.

In some instances children may be confined for long periods of time, and their parents or caregivers cannot be with them around the clock. Perhaps you and your children can offer to drop in and read to the patient if the staff approves.

If boxed games are available, play a quiet game with the patient if his condition allows. When the patient begins to feel better, you may want to supply a coloring book and crayons or some other similar activity.

In situations in which hospital policy does not allow children to visit sick children, ask for suggestions from the staff. Make some suggestions of your own so that the staff will understand the scope of what you are prepared to do. For example, you and your children may offer to make banners or posters and bring balloons to honor a child who is observing a birthday. Or you may offer to bring crafts items which your children have made and have an attendant place items on meal trays on a special date, such as July 4.

If you discover a child who is terminally ill, you may want to ask for guidance from church staff or a social services staff person. Your children may need to be excluded from visitation in cases such as these.

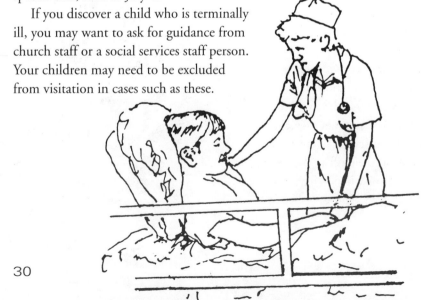

PLANT A TREE IN HONOR OF A MISSIONARY

Make your children ecology-conscious, as well as keep the name of a particular missionary before them as they grow up, by planting a tree seedling that will grow well in your environment. Let the children help make the selection of the missionary or missionary family and help select the perfect tree from the nursery.

Make planting day a special time by planning a few simple things to do. First, find out about the missionary whom you are seeking to honor and remember. If you can find a picture of the missionary in a publication, plan to show it as you tell some facts about what the missionary does on his or her missions field. Give the tree the name of the missionary. For example say, "We will call this our Missionary John Doe Tree." Plan to take a snapshot of the children as they help to plant and water the tree. Plan to make a duplicate of the best picture so that you can send a copy to the missionary for whom the tree is to be named. Along with the snapshot include the assurance that your family will make a regular practice of remembering him or her in prayer.

After the tree has been planted, establish a watering schedule and let the children take turns with the watering. Accompany the children to the tree frequently and see that it is cared for properly. Always call the name of the missionary for whom the tree is named and tell recent information about what the missionary is doing.

MAKE NOTE CARDS TO SEND

Combine a practical crafts project with an environmental concept. Look around the house for some paper which can be recycled and used to make homemade note cards. If you do not find what you need, purchase some plain paper which bears the recycled symbol. Purchase envelopes that are also made from recycled paper. Purchase postage stamps that have an environmental theme.

Lead the children to research information and pictures about endangered animals. Furnish water-based markers or other art media. Prepare an area where the children can paint or draw their versions of endangered species on the front panels of several homemade greeting cards. The children may choose their own credit lines and make-believe trademarks for the back panels. The inside panels should be reserved for the message area unless the children want to make tiny illustrations down one margin.

If you find that one of the cards is exceptionally well done, you may want to take it to a quick-print company and get duplicates made at a relatively low cost. Try for a color reproduction if the cost is acceptable.

Decide how to use the cards to accomplish a missions purpose. Help the children make a list of prospects for their Sunday School class or other church group. Help the children with the message writing, addressing, stamping, and mailing.

MINISTRY THROUGH CORRESPONDENCE

Many issues of the daily news bear accounts of heartbreak and trauma. Although we may not know many of the persons who are thrust into the middle of bad conditions, we are touched by their needs. Sometimes it is within our power to help in tangible ways, in addition to praying for the persons.

Your family can begin a ministry to persons who make the headlines because of their adversities. Openly express compassion for the persons in front of your children so that they can see that you feel compassion and Christian concern. Ask your children what they would say to comfort the person if they were to meet the person face to face. Refine the comments and express them in a note of comfort and encouragement. Perhaps your children can select a favorite Bible verse to include at the bottom of the note.

If the news notice did not give a mailing address, you may be able to find the address by checking the phone book or a city directory at the public library. You may choose to sign the note without including your return address, depending upon the nature of the situation.

If an appeal for specific help was publicized along with the news report, discuss with your family some possible responses you can make. Lead your family to remember the person until his crisis has passed.

FAMILY HOME BURNS!

Last night a blaze engulfed the home of a local resident ,Wanita de Latoya. Neighbors said they heard an explotion shortly after midnight.All occupants evacuated the area shortly after they heard the noise. Fire Marshal,Adam Bolden, said :"the cause of the explosion has not been identified as of this time"; all thoughs wishing to help the family should contact First Baptist (

MAKE A SUNSHINE BASKET

Spray a small container with bright yellow paint. When the basket or other container is dry, allow the children to add festive trim or decals.

With a recipient in mind, lead the children to plan what to include in the basket. Make a list of items, such as sample sizes of packaged foods, individual servings of juices, pocket packs of facial tissues, ballpoint pen, notepad, blank note cards, and an item which can be wrapped and labeled as a mystery gift to be opened on a certain day.

If possible, include some homemade items in the collection. For instance, the children might enjoy making a calendar for the coming month and writing a Bible verse on each of the spaces where the dates appear. A small bottle of water can be tucked into the middle of the items and a fresh blossom or two from your flower garden can piggy back in the sunshine basket.

Make plans to deliver the basket at the convenience of the recipient. If your children cannot accompany you to deliver the basket, be sure to relay greetings and best wishes from them and tell the recipient that the children helped to arrange the basket.

During the visit, perform a ministry of listening and pray with the person if he or she seems to be open to prayer. A few days after the visit, telephone and inquire about the person's general well-being. Continue showing interest as appropriate.

BE AWARE OF WORLD HUNGER

Unfortunately, the bounty of summer's fruit does not extend to all the world. Make your family more conscious and concerned about people in countries where famine and political upheaval have contributed to hunger.

From missions periodicals and environmental news releases, collect facts that you can use to inform your family of the need to conserve, give to the support of world hunger funds, and pray for solutions to hunger problems.

Find out what your church does to help relieve world hunger. If there is to be a special offering, lead your family to decide how much money you will give to the offering. For several days or weeks prior to the time for the offering, set aside small amounts of money until you have met your goal.

Since rice is a food which is sent to many of the deprived nations, consider using a "rice bowl" in which to set aside the family's collection. The children can make a bank from a plastic container with a lid that can be slit. They may apply a coating of white glue to the lid after the money slit has been cut. Then they may sprinkle a single layer of rice onto the glue and allow it to dry. If they wish, they may use art paper to cover the trade name on the dish part of the container and label the container "Our Family's Offering for World Hunger."

Find out when the offering is to be turned in to the church. If the offering is to be placed into an envelope, convert coins into bills or a check before making the offering.

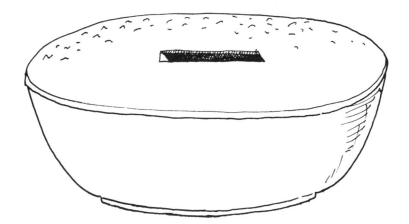

PLAN A PIÑATA PARTY

Build a children's social around a missions theme. If you wish, send written invitations with a Mexican motif. For refreshments consider chips and dip, tacos or burritos, and fried ice cream. Serve soft drinks in brightly-colored disposable cups. Provide matching or coordinated paper products and table covering. In the area where the group will play games, suspend a piñata as the main decoration. Use a sombrero as a centerpiece on the refreshment table.

If you can locate a recording or a tape of children's music with a Mexican sound, check it out from a library. Encourage your children to help with the selection of games to play. Consult resources such as *A Carousel of Countries* or *Fun Around the World* by Mary Kinney Branson, published by New Hope Press, Birmingham, Alabama.

Near the closing of the party, explain the significance of the piñata as a traditional party thrill in Mexico. Comment briefly that we have a missions interest in our neighbors to the south. Finally, allow the children to take turns wearing a blindfold and trying to strike the piñata with a bat-like object. Caution the observers to stand clear of the child whose turn it is to swing the stick. Continue until the piñata breaks, spilling its contents.

FIELD TRIP WITH A WORLD VIEW

It has been said that the world has come to our doorstep. Your children are likely to live in an environment that is more like a mosaic of cultures than any other generation of Americans who have gone before us. Equip your children to understand the religious views of persons with non-Christian backgrounds.

Look in your local newspapers for listings of meeting places of persons of eastern religious groups, such as Buddhists and Hindus. Also find out about various Jewish congregations in your area. Perhaps you will want to locate a congregation of Christian Jews, also.

Find out when you may tour the meeting place of the group you select. Inquire about the nature of the tour and be aware of how long the tour will take. Make a reservation if it is necessary.

Become somewhat knowledgeable of the basic beliefs of the religious group and inform your children of some of those beliefs. Be sure to point out that all of the groups except the Christian Jews do not believe in Jesus as their Saviour. Perhaps you would like to talk with your children ahead of time and make a list of questions they would like to ask. Remind the children that missionaries go to other countries to tell persons of these religions about Jesus.

MUSIC OF OTHER CULTURES

Lead your children to develop an appreciation for other cultures by becoming familiar with some of the children's songs of other lands. Go to the media section of your public library and ask for several recordings or tapes of music of other lands. Perhaps the librarian will be able to advise you of particular albums which will appeal to your children.

Plan a family event around an international theme. Perhaps the music can be played as background to a special meal with an international flair. Select one country for the focus or plan a potpourri of tasty foods from several countries. For example, the appetizer may be representative of one country, the main course of another country, and the dessert of yet another country.

Tell the children that missionaries to other countries must become accustomed to the foods and the culture. There is much to learn when one becomes a missionary.

Language is another cultural element that missionaries need to cope with. If some of the musical selections have foreign language lyrics, check the album cover or cassette label to see whether there is a copy of the lyrics. If some of your musical selections are appropriate for the children to learn, play the selections again following the meal and help the children learn to sing songs, such as "*La Cucaracha*" or "*Frere Jacques.*"

PRAY FOR WORLD PEACE

The cry for peace knows no one season. Somewhere in the world at this moment there are people who long for peace in their land and in their lives. Be a part of their deliverance through prayer.

Lead the family to watch for current news events in the media which demonstrate a need for peace. Develop a prayer calendar in behalf of specific nations and individuals who need relief from oppression and turmoil. If you have a world globe or a world atlas, mark the locations of the persons for whom the family will pray each day for a specific period of time. If there are several points of agony at this time, perhaps older children and adult family members will volunteer to pray specifically for one of the points of need.

As you pray, include the missionaries and their families who are working in locations where there is danger or other deprivations. If you have a directory which lists the names and locations of missionaries, scan it and make a separate list of names of missionaries who need special care and comfort at this time.

Continue to pray daily until you get reports that problems have been resolved. Follow up your prayers with letters of concern to missionaries and others whom you may know in the troubled areas.

HAWAIIAN LUAU FOR PASTOR'S FAMILY

Perhaps it has been a while since you have expressed appreciation to your pastor and his family for setting the pace for outreach and ministry in your community. Plan an event for this summer with that purpose in mind.

Your deck, patio, or family room can be decorated with an island theme. Watch the garage sales and party stores for festive Hawaiian items to use in your party. A supply of colorful plastic leis, cut flowers, slices of fresh pineapple, patio torches, and recorded music of the islands will blend in with almost any menu that you wish to prepare.

Let the children help with the preparations, especially the decorating and planning of the traditional greeting with the leis. An older child may be put in charge of keeping the music playing throughout the meal.

Check with the pastor to find out when the calendar is clear for your event. Follow up with a homemade invitation that carries a Hawaiian theme. If your family plans to dress in casual clothing similar to island attire, invite the pastor's family to wear clothing appropriate to the theme.

At some point during the meal, honor the pastor for a specific outreach or ministry task that he has performed recently. Decide on what will be said and who will say it. If someone in the family is good at writing poetry, perhaps someone else will be able to read the poetic tribute.

VISIT MISSIONARIES AT THEIR STATIONS

This summer your family may be planning to get away for a few days on a long-awaited vacation. As you plan your schedule, consider making missions memories by looking up a missionary's place of service and calling ahead to ask whether you and the family can drop by to tour the site or possibly attend a service or some other missions event.

Perhaps you know some missionaries personally and can include them on your list of people to drop in on for remembering old times. Take into consideration the work schedule of the individual missionaries because their summer schedules are usually extremely busy. The visit, although brief, can give your family an insight into the daily life and work of a "real live" missionary.

Depending upon the circumstances, perhaps you could make a videotape or at least make a few snapshots of some of the projects the missionary is engaged in this summer. If the missionary relates specific needs, encourage him and promise your prayer support.

During the brief visit be sure to include the children in the conversation and discussion. Ask the children whether they have any questions they would like to ask. Conclude the tour or visit with a genuine expression of appreciation for the time the missionary has spent with your family. Get the complete mailing address of the Mission station so that you may correspond later on special occasions.

GIVE A SINGLE PARENT A TREAT

Some single parents find that their summer schedule is just a bit more demanding than the rest of the year. The children are out of school, of course, and that means extra planning to meet the children's needs.

If your church does not have a program to assist the single parents of your area, consider what you may be able to do to help at least one single parent and his or her children experience a treat. Listen for expressed needs, such as transportation to and from swimming lessons or some other events. Enlist your own children in befriending the children in special ways. Perhaps there will be a need for a sitter for one particular time when the usual day care plans do not work out. Or perhaps the children will need someone to call in case of an emergency, and you are willing to be on call for such a purpose.

If the single parent becomes ill, perhaps you could take in some food for the children so that the parent can have a few extra moments for rest and recovery. If you know that the single parent does not take the children to church on Sunday, or if the parent does not have time off to see that the children get to attend church-sponsored summer events, seek to make arrangements for transportation. If your church has a bus ministry, perhaps the parent might give consent for the bus to stop and pick up his or her children.

If you detect spiritual needs which you do not feel qualified to address, refer the parent to your pastor or minister to singles. Encourage single parents who are giving their best to the nurturing of their children and support them in your prayers.

ILLUSTRATE FAMILY'S PLAN OF GIVING

Plan a demonstration to help your children understand concepts, such as planned giving, tithing, and missions offerings. Rehearse this demonstration before using it to explain to the children how you determine what part of the family income will be given through your church's plan of giving.

If you wish, you may use money from a board game your children have or pieces of green paper. Decide how many play-money bills to set out to represent gross income for the period of time you choose. On a scrap of paper write *Money Earned* and place the label by the bills. On another scrap of paper write *Living Expenses*. With a piece of yarn, circle the number of bills that represent the percentage of the gross income used for living expenses. Make a label for *Tithe*. With a piece of yarn of another color, circle one-tenth of the bills. Make a label that reads *Missions Offerings*. With yarn of another color, circle the bills that represent the percentage of income your family gives to special missions offerings.

When you are ready, demonstrate to the children how your family uses its income for living and for giving. As the children think about these concepts, perhaps they will have questions you will want to discuss with them.

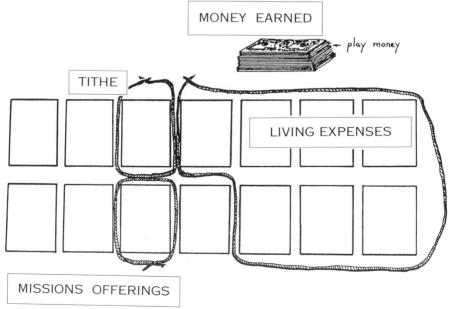

43

SAVE VALUABLE TRASH FOR CHARITY

In many cities some of the social agencies collect valuable trash and other items in order to raise extra money for special projects. Find out what is being done in your area and arrange to take part in the effort.

Perhaps the center for the homeless has a drop-off point for items, such as aluminum cans, glass bottles, or other recyclables. Perhaps a senior citizens' center has need of some throw-away materials to use in a crafts project they have underway.

Encourage your children to remember to save the needed items. Use this as an opportunity to show that it is good to learn how to be creative with things some people usually throw away. Also, show the children that it is good to share small things as well as large things to help others.

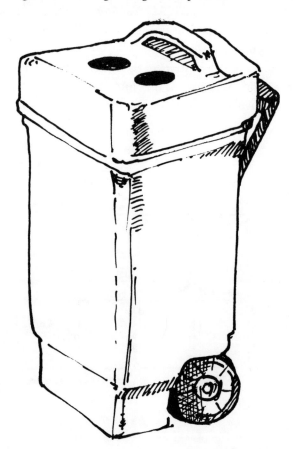

EXTEND A SMILE AND A HELPING HAND

If your church or a neighborhood facility has a day-care center, find out whether they would welcome a special treat from you and your family. As you investigate what is permitted at the day care center, you may need to be specific about what you have in mind as your project.

Perhaps your helping hand can go beyond a cupcake treat or some other simple food that most children enjoy. If you or your children have a special family talent, you may offer to bring your "show" to the day-care center. Your children might enjoy dressing up as some characters in a children's story and pantomiming as you read or tell the story. Of course, you and the children would need to refine your presentation before taking your show on the road!

If you have puppets, perhaps you can prepare a brief puppet show for the preschoolers at the day care center. Your children can help with the puppet show, too.

You might offer to take your "Singing Von Who's It Family" children's favorite fun-song program for a 15-minute music appreciation experience.

Whatever you choose to do, you may approach the experience as a fun time for your children as well as for the children of the day-care center. Take the opportunity to show your support to the day-care staff who faithfully perform their role of Christian caregivers to some very important people—the children at the day-care center.

BACK-TO-SCHOOL SUPPLIES FOR A MISSION CENTER

If there is an inner-city mission near you, perhaps they have need of a new stash of supplies for the beginning of their new school year. After-school programs and day-care programs in inner-city missions often reach children who cannot or do not have access to basic supplies needed to help them develop readiness skills and so forth.

Contact the director of the mission or whatever facility you wish to help and let your willingness be known. After you get approval, shop smart and deliver your gift in a useful container. Of course, your children should be included in each phase of this helpful project.

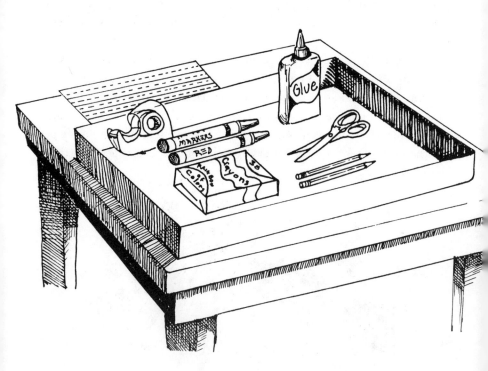

FALL

Someone has said that if you repeat an action 30 times you will have established a habit. That is what fall is like for many of us. It is a time to get into a groove. We put aside the spontaneity and relaxation of summer and establish, or reestablish, habits.

Fall can be a time to make choices, particularly if your children are school-age. You can face a myriad of activities and opportunities. What do you sign up for? What do you eliminate? How do you separate the best from the good or the bad?

Unfortunately, scheduled activities can eat away at family time. Crammed calendars can so control you and your family that you have little or no opportunity to devote time and energy to a missions life-style.

Can this fall be different? Is there a better time to establish habits and memories that reflect a balanced Christian life-style? Think about memories your children will take with them from a typical fall. Will they remember a life lived in the car with multiple stops and frantic dashes to assorted activities? Or will they remember times of thinking about and helping others?

As you plan your fall activities, save time for spontaneous acts of ministry to people God puts in your family's path. Save time for making missions memories. Leave a legacy of memories for your children by making time together and time for others a habit.

"He has caused his wonders to be remembered; the Lord is gracious and compassionate."

(Psalm 111:4 NIV)

TOGETHER CAN BE BETTER

In many towns this is the season when thoughts turn to feeding the home-less and building food supplies that will be dontated to needy families when the winter winds begin to howl and some breadwinners no longer have earn-ing power because of their seasonal jobs. Watch the newspapers and TV ads for requests that are likely to be urgent. Check your resources to determine what you and your family can budget for sharing with one or more of the agencies in your community.

Find out whether your favorite agency has need of small, large, or restau-rant-size canned foods. Do they accept canned foods only, or will boxes and bagged staples be accepted, also? Do they need baby food? If so, what vari-eties? What about formula for babies? Are food supplements for the elderly appropriate? Are certain diet foods needed? What are the rules about shelf-life of the products accepted?

These questions are not intended to become barriers or blockades, rather they are questions to ask agencies which may not always publish a complete list of their needs. Many agencies will accept almost anything they are given, but why not hit the target of need as you give? Be a good mission scout by being prepared to give the best!

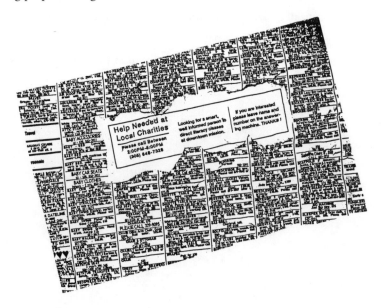

TELL ABOUT JESUS

Even your young children probably are familiar with the term *show and tell.* The term will help with one easy approach for teaching your children how to develop a natural approach to telling their friends about their best friend, Jesus. Lead your children to understand that Jesus' command to tell others about Him was not a casual request, but that it is an order that followers of Jesus must obey.

Tell your children that as they obey Jesus' rules, they will be showing others that they know about Jesus. By telling about Jesus, the children can give others an opportunity to make Jesus their best friend, too.

Lead your children to develop skills in telling stories about Jesus. Begin with the story of Jesus' birth and continue with several of the main events in Jesus' life and ministry, including some of His miracles and some of the important things He taught His friends. Story by story, lead your children to recall and tell what they know about Jesus, including the fact that Jesus is God's Son, the Saviour. Be sure that they are able to tell each story in a manner appropriate to their age level. As the children tell and retell the stories at home, they can develop the ability to tell about Jesus with ease and grace. When the children are older and have become Christians, they will be more likely to be witnesses to their faith.

MAKE A CURIO COLLECTION

Many homes display mementos of their travels and special family events. Some parents and grandparents have collected curios from faraway places and are keeping them tucked away almost forgotten. In this age of expanded free world trade, many homes have items made in other countries. Some of the items are representative of cultures of other lands. To help your children become more aware of people of other lands where missionaries tell about Jesus, find some curios and set them up in a special cabinet or shelf in your home. Use the items as attention getters and conversation starters with your family. Be sure that your children understand the significance of each item.

Grandparents and great-grandparents may want to help you in your search for curios such as these. Perhaps there are some interesting missions adventure stories behind some of the curios that have been in the family for a long time. From now on when anyone in your church or family plans to go on a volunteer missions trip, consider sending along some cash for the purchase of at least one item to add to your missions curio collection. The collection need not be costly in order to serve the purpose of missions awareness. A miniature flag collection or a foreign postage stamp collection can serve the purpose if more expensive items are not affordable.

INTERNATIONAL ATTIRE

When you hear the "Mom, what can we do now?" question the next time, here is a surprise you can pull out of your fabric scraps and remnants. Show the children some ideas for making some clothing items like people in other countries wear. Here are three ideas that are simple enough for preschoolers, yet challenging for younger children, also.

Introduce an item that is worn by the *gauchos* (cowboys) in Argentina as well as in other Latin countries. The *sarape* is a rectangular piece of fabric which is sometimes fringed on the two ends. See the illustration for how to cut a *sarape* to wear across the shoulder.

Your girls may enjoy making some shawls like the women and girls of Latin countries often wear. The illustration of the shawl indicates a triangular piece of fabric cut to fit over the shoulders and slightly tuck under the arms. Edges may be fringed on the two edges leading to the point on the triangle.

A third idea comes from India and is appropriate for girls. The *sari* is a wrap-and-tuck garment which is wound around the body as shown in the illustration. The basic garment under the *sari* is similar to a simple, sleeveless blouse. Sandals or thongs can be worn with the *sari*.

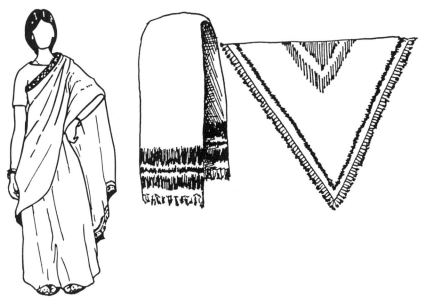

RENT A FILM ABOUT MISSIONS AREA

Although many younger children may be exposed to world news reports about stress points around the world, some do not make the connection that these faraway places are the same places they hear about in their missions education groups at church. Help to create world awareness and the reality of those faraway places through the use of video in your home.

Although you may not be able to rent a missions education videotape, perhaps you can rent a videotape about a country in which your denomination sponsors missionaries. Check with the missions education director in your church or your church media librarian for suggestions. Otherwise, go to the media section of your public library and check out a videotape about life in an African country or another country in which you are certain that missionaries are telling about Jesus.

If you check out a commercially prepared videotape, preview it and select portions of the tape that are appropriate for viewers the age of your children. Plan a time to view the tape with the children. Explain why you selected the tape and how it relates to the life and work of missionaries in that country.

Later as you find opportunity to talk about something you saw in the videotape or mention the name of a missionary to that country, it will be easier for your children to visualize what life is like in that particular country. An activity such as this can help your children develop an appreciation for other cultures as well as develop missions awareness.

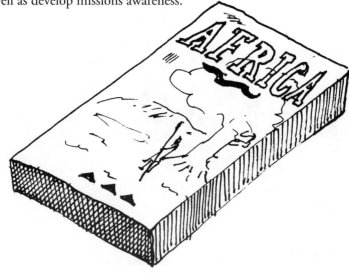

SNACKS FROM AROUND THE WORLD

When your children are bringing friends home with them, you may want to set out some snacks from around the world. You may want to label the foods or you may simply identify the foods for the children.

Arrange a tray with samples of several of these items:

- Sauerkraut and wieners—Germany
- Spaghetti—Italy
- Mini kabobs—Samoa, Tonga, or other Polynesian islands
- Nachos and jalapeno dip—Mexico
- Stir-fry veggies with cashews—Orient
- Fried Irish potatoes—Ireland
- German potato salad—Germany
- Pastry—France
- Cheese—Switzerland
- Swedish apple cake—Sweden
- Mandarin oranges—China
- Guacamole salad—Mexico
- Chocolate fondue—France
- Miniature quiche—France

If these suggestions do not suit your taste buds, look in a cookbook or see a resource, such as *Guess What I Made!?!* by Sharlande Sledge, New Hope, or *Look, I'm Cooking! (Simple Recipes for Preschoolers)* by Barbara Owen, New Hope.

For beverages, you may serve an American pop or an English tea. Select something appropriate for the rest of the snack menu you have chosen.

As you invite children to the table, you may want to speak in a foreign language or speak with your best stage accent. Introduce the children to the tasting experience, relating the morsels to a few brief facts about familiar customs that accompany the use of a particular food in the country it represents.

ENCOURAGE LITERACY

Assisting internationals with literacy skills is an important missions venture. Find out whether your congregation sponsors a literacy ministry. If a program is underway, find out how you and your family can assist. If there is not an ongoing program in your church, check with neighborhood groups who are assisting children, youth, and adults in improving their reading and writing skills. Find out how to receive instruction for how to become a tutor. Investigate ways to become involved in established groups, such as adult education centers and social services centers.

After receiving tutorial instruction, you may want to volunteer to meet weekly with a regularly assigned student. In some literacy systems it is believed to be most effective to employ the one-to-one teacher-pupil ratio. If you must teach more than one student, be sure that the students are about the same level in reading and writing ability. Your instruction materials may advise you to begin at the basic level and discover how fast and how far your students can progress. In that way you can help the more advanced students correct minor difficulties in language skills.

In some cases your students may ask you to help them master important material, such as naturalization manuals or drivers' manuals.

Normally, literacy tutors do not make aggressive Christian witness to persons who are not open to Christian teachings. However, through patience and service you can model a Christian spirit. You may be privileged to answer the student's first questions about your religion. Be prepared.

SHOWER FOR CHILDREN'S HOME

In many states there are several children's homes. Find out where the nearest children's home is located and find out more about the facility. If the children's home is church-sponsored, find out who the contact person is and ask her what kinds of items are needed at the present time. If you prefer, suggest that you would like to give a selection of games for the children to play indoors during the late fall and winter. Ask the contact person to find out which games are preferred.

Be a smart shopper and look for appropriate games at sale prices. If you have access to previously owned games that show no wear, you may want to combine them with your newly purchased games. Of course, you would not want to put any of your children's games with your shower items without their willingness to give up the games.

If the children's home is organized in a cottage format, you may want to provide a shower for only one cottage. Find out the ages and sexes of the children who live in the cottage. Perhaps you would like to give school supplies, a variety of breakfast cereal, or restaurant-size cans of fruit. Shopping for a special surprise that will thrill the residents of the home can be a family project.

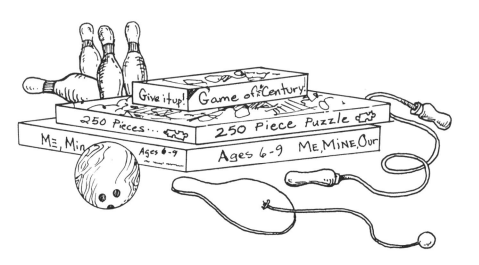

CALL A FAMILY PALAVER

Explain to the children that in some African countries the people use drums to call the people to important meetings. The meeting is called a *palaver* [pah-la-ver].

Guide your children to make some drums from large coffee cans or other containers which can have vinyl laced over each open end. The sides of the drums can be decorated like those you find pictured in missions periodicals or a reliable source, such as *National Geographic*.

Select some articles about missions in Africa and read the information. Be prepared to tell the information in a manner appropriate for the ages of your children. Plan to make a clearing in the middle of a room where the drummers and the family can sit around an imaginary campfire.

After dinner one evening, tell the family that when they hear the sounds of the drums, they must gather for a *palaver*. Show the younger children how to

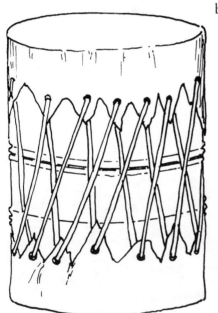

beat the drums and chant, "Come, come, come, come to the *pah-la-ver*." The drumming and chanting should continue until the family comes into the room. Set the example by sitting cross-legged and inviting the other family members to sit in a circle.

Begin the *palaver* by explaining that everyone is to pretend that they are in an African country at an important tribal meeting. Then say, "These are some things that are happening in our country now." Continue as you tell your missions information as though you are the chief of the tribe. At the conclusion, encourage the children to ask questions about the information you told. Conclude with prayer for the missionaries mentioned in the missions information you used as your source.

A MAKE-BELIEVE MISSIONS TRIP

You probably would not want to take your children on a missions trip to a jungle or to a remote corner of the world, but you can familiarize them with what it would be like to take such an exciting trip.

First, decide on a country where your make-believe trip will be. Find out what you can about the culture of the country, the kinds of missions work done there, the kinds of foods available, housing and clothing used, and mode of travel commonly used.

If possible, take your children to a travel agency and get brochures and travel posters about the country where your make-believe trip will take you. Explain to the agent that this is an educational experience for your children rather than an actual trip. Perhaps the agent will have time to give the children some travel tips which will make the experience more memorable.

For the next several days, lead the children to pretend to be on the trip. The overseas plane trip can be played out in rows of chairs in your family room. One of the older children can role-play the part of a stewardess. A tour of the country can be a walk around the neighborhood as you tell what you have learned from the travel brochures. Back at home, you may boil drinking water and pitch tents for the night. Other props and activities can be included in keeping with what you discovered in your research. Throughout the make-believe experience, lead the children to realize why missionaries go to other countries to tell about Jesus.

INCLUDE SINGLE PERSONS
IN THANKSGIVING DAY PLANS

Get in touch with the director of the singles ministry in your congregation. Find out about one or two single persons who will not be going to relatives' Thanksgiving gatherings this year. Ask the minister to introduce you to the single persons if you do not know them. At least two weeks before Thanksgiving Day invite the potential guests and allow them time to check their calendars before you get back to them by phone. If the persons must decline your invitation, invite other single persons. Remember that singles can be found in more than one age group.

Prepare your younger children to be pleasant cohosts by giving them specific assignments of what they can do to make the guests feel welcomed and have a good holiday with your family. Help the children realize what kinds of questions they can ask the guests during the Thanksgiving meal. Also make suggestions of things the children can discuss at the table and afterward during the visit.

Decide how many of your regular family traditions you will keep at the upcoming event. Decide whether you will begin a new tradition, such as taking turns naming something for which each person is particularly thankful for this year or singing the blessing, using the familiar "Doxology."

Let the children assist with meal plans and preparation and in making place cards for the table.

EXPERIENCE
FOREIGN LANGUAGE MISSIONS

Tell your children that missionaries who work in countries where languages other than English are spoken must learn other languages. Missionaries must learn to read the Bible and preach and teach in the languages the people of those countries understand.

Lead the children to understand a little about the process of learning Bible verses in other languages. Select a brief verse for younger children and select longer passages for older children. You may copy the following verses on index cards so that the children can have easy access to the verses while they are learning to pronounce the words and perhaps memorize the verses. If you read other languages, you may add other verses to these verses from the Spanish translation.

"Dios es amor" (1 Juan 4:8 Spanish).
[Dee-os ayes ah-more]

"Porque de tal manera amo Dios al mundo, que dio a su Hijo unico, para que toda aquel que cree en el, no perezca, mas tenga vida eterna" (Juan 3:16, Spanish).

[PORE-kay day tahl mah-NAY-rah ah-MOE dee-OS ahl MOON-doe, keh dee-O ah sue E-ho OO-nee-ko, PAH-rah keh TOE-dah ah-KEL keh KRAY-e ayn el, no pay-RAY-skah, mahs TANG-ah VI-dah a-TER-nah.]

MISSIONS MATH PROBLEM

Lead your older children to work a missions math problem and demonstrate it for your younger children. Use current information available in missions journals, prayer calendars, or missions periodicals.

Use marbles of two colors or buttons of two colors to complete this math problem. Let a marble of one color stand for an individual missionary in a particular country. From your sources of missions information, find out how many missionaries your denomination sponsors in a particular country. Also find out what the non-Christian population of that country is at the present time.

Lead the older children to decide how many thousands or millions of non-Christians will be represented by each marble. Then lead the children to discover how many missionaries there are in that country. Lead the children to discuss some of the problems the ratio of missionaries to non-Christians is likely to present. If you wish, you may expand this activity by finding the ratio of missionaries to non-Christians in another country.

Lead the children to discuss some of the implications that arise out of such ratios as those demonstrated. Ask the children what Christians are supposed to do to improve the ratios. If they do not know how to respond, suggest things, such as giving more money to missions, sending Bibles to missionaries, supporting volunteers who go to help career missionaries, and praying for missionaries who have much work to do every day.

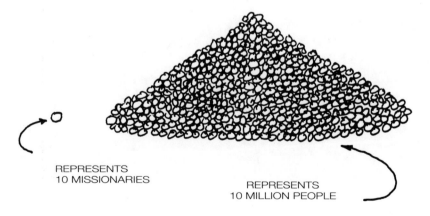

REPRESENTS
10 MISSIONARIES

REPRESENTS
10 MILLION PEOPLE

WRITE TO A CHILD OF MISSIONARIES

Sometimes people refer to missionaries' children as MKs, short for "missionaries' kids." MKs are scattered around the world, living in uncommon circumstances, experiencing life unlike most American children find their day-to-day happenings. Some MKs know more about the country in which they now live than they know about the United States.

Show the MKs that Christians back home are aware that they exist and that they are valuable to the missions cause where their parents are working. Get names, overseas addresses, and ages of some MKs. Perhaps there may be missionary families from your area who have MKs with whom your older children can correspond.

Discover information about the MKs, such as birthdays, hobbies, favorite sports, favorite kinds of books and videotapes, and so forth. Remember the MKs on their birthdays and other important holidays. Be aware of special prayer needs of the MKs and their parents. Be supportive of MKs who are away from their parents, attending boarding school in adjoining countries.

Encourage your children to develop their skills at corresponding, keeping an upbeat attitude, and keeping the MKs up-to-date on things of interest to Christian boys and girls the ages of the MKs. Decide on a frequency for the correspondence, check on the amount of overseas postage, and find out about any other postal regulations of the country where the MKs live.

Follow up on the penpal arrangement when the MKs return to the United States. Plan to meet and perhaps entertain the MKs if possible.

MAKE DOORKNOB HANGERS

Help your children become more aware that for Christians, helping others is a mandate. Lead the children to look up the following Bible references in a modern version of the Bible, selecting verses to use on doorknob hangers. You may supplement this list with your favorite verses about helping and serving others. Matthew 7:12; 10:8*b*; 19:19*b*; 25:40; Luke 6:31; John 13:15.

"Do to others as you would have them do to you" (Luke 6:31, NIV).

Choose a durable paper, such as lightweight poster board or the board that you have saved from hosiery and undergarment packages. Cut the board into four-by-eight-inch pieces. Cut a hole and a slash as illustrated.

Explain to the children that they can make door-knob hangers to use as reminders to help others and to use as gifts. Provide colored, water-based markers for the children to use to write the verses and illustrate the edges of the knob hangers. As the children work on the knob hangers, talk with them about ways to apply the verses.

Lead the children to decide where they will place the hangers and to whom they will present some of the hangers. Also, lead the children to decide on specific ways to apply the verses as they help specific people.

MAKE A FRIENDSHIP THROW

If your children have an adopted grandparent, lead the children to plan to make a lap throw for the special friend to use this fall and winter. Let each child make a sketch of something he would like to put on the miniature quilt. The sketch should be made on paper so the child can get the results he wants before he starts. Use fabric markers to make the sketch on the cloth that will be used as the quilt top.

Follow these steps as you lead the children to make the lap throw. Older children may be able to help you with the last steps, also.

LEARN HOW AND WHEN TO ASSIST DISABLED PERSONS

Some disabled persons seem to have a spirit of independence and self-confidence. Some persons do not want strangers to offer to assist them with doors, packages, hazards, and so forth. Others gladly accept any offer of assistance. All disabled persons appreciate being recognized as normal persons with the exception of their handicap. All persons, disabled or not, want to be known by name and known for all the many things they can accomplish. Plan to lead your children to develop a positive attitude toward persons who are normal with that one exception commonly known as a handicap.

Talk with mature persons in your congregation who have a diversity of physical impairments and ask them what kinds of assistance is acceptable and unacceptable to offer. Explain that you are trying to teach your children to be responsible, caring persons who know what they should and should not do as they relate to children and adults with physical impairments. Take notes so that you can report to your children. If your children are older, they may have other questions you can ask your expert to help you answer. Express appreciation for the advice you get.

INTERVIEW A MISSIONARY

Find out whether there is a career missionary or missions volunteer in your area. Lead your family to make a list of interview questions you would like to ask the missionary.

Make an appointment for the interview. If it is appropriate, take your children for the interview visit. Otherwise, ask permission to take to the interview the list of interview questions, a camera (videocamera if possible), or a cassette recorder. If you will be interviewing a career missionary who is on furlough, be thoughtful of the missionary's time schedule because he will have many things to do while on furlough. There perhaps will be more flexibility in the schedule of the volunteer missionary whom you may choose to interview.

If your children do not have sufficient questions, you may suggest questions, such as:

1. What was your feeling when you first reached the place where you would work as a missionary? Have your feelings changed? If so, how?
2. What has been the best part of your missions experience?
3. What kinds of things do you do each day that you do not have to do in the United States?
4. Do you get mail from Christians in the United States? Do you get packages from home?
5. Where do the missionary children attend school?

MAKE A PERMANENT FLOWER ARRANGEMENT

With the advent of fall there is a flurry of activity in the great, colorful outdoors. When we see furry little animals packing in their food supplies for the cold days ahead, we get in the mood to save some of summer's goodness, too. You can plan to share some of your fall treasures with the homebound.

Take the children on a nature hunt in an area where collecting is not against the law. Natural things, such as wild fern, moss, dried seed pods, reeds, nuts, sycamore fruit, fruit from a *Bois de'Arc* tree, and pinecones can be arranged into lovely fall arrangements. Collect a variety of usable items.

Clean up the items, remove broken stems, and decide on how to arrange gifts to take to homebounds. Baskets, pottery, and glass containers can be used for your arrangements. Guide the children to assist according to their ability. Find a job for everyone. Enlist one child to write the gift tags to accompany the arrangements.

Make an appointment for the visits you will make. Take the children with you to deliver the arrangements and visit briefly with the homebound.

OFFER TRANSPORTATION
TO CHILDREN

Even in the day of going to outer space and flying at the speed of sound there are some transportation needs you may be able to remedy. When you discover children whose parents do not take them to Sunday School, you may want to offer to transport the children each week.

In communicating with the parents and prospective children, you may assume that the parents need to know more about you and your family and your intentions. You may also assume that the parents need to know about the routine you have for your family, including time to be ready, where you attend Sunday School, expectations during the worship service, and when you will return the children home. Parents may want to ask other questions, such as will the children be pressured to join your church, will you supervise them during the worship service, will they be expected to bring an offering, and what should they wear.

Perhaps you will need to make reminder phone calls for a while. You may be disappointed if the parents do not cooperate in getting the children ready on time. Although there are sometimes numerous setbacks to an activity such as this, much can be gained from sharing transportation with those who will accept. Remain faithful in your dedication to reaching out in the name of Christ to the children who need this ministry.

VOLUNTEER AT A MISSIONS CENTER

Thanksgiving Day at mission points in your city may be cause for additional volunteer assistance. People from professions, offices, and other occupations sometimes muster at the serving line at their local rescue mission. Some of the same volunteers appear year after year because of the blessing they get from serving a wonderful meal to persons who need a place to eat on such a special day.

Make plans for a different schedule for your own traditional holiday observance so that you and as many of your family as appropriate can pitch in with the big task of preparing and serving at the mission. Mature teenagers and young adults are almost certain to find jobs they can perform.

A week or two before Thanksgiving Day, call the mission and ask what kinds of help they will need before, during, and after the meal.

Once you have your job description in mind, dress appropriately for your involvement, whether it is peeling potatoes, setting tables, filling plates, clearing tables, or whatever. Also, prepare your mind and spirit for the day. Remember to be kind, cheerful, and generous. If you and your family are inexperienced at this type service, follow the example of other volunteers who seem to know their way around the mission setting.

BEFRIEND A TEENAGER

Some teenagers seem not to have a significant adult in their lives to whom they can turn for sound advice when they have such need. If there is such a teenager in your circle of acquaintances, you and your family may assist in providing an anchor during a difficult time.

A ministry of listening may be needed. Be prepared to keep confidences and withhold advice unless you are asked for specific information. If you feel that the teenager needs to have expert help, suggest to the teenager the name of the person who can help.

If the teenager is seeking a support system because of a deficient self-concept, use your best judgment in providing praise and encouragement. If the teenager has academic needs, supply tutoring according to your abilities.

If the teenager has a special talent which has gone unnoticed by his own family, help him channel the talent into opportunities for further development. Consider helping the teenager become involved in a supportive group at your church.

Watch for ways to encourage a youth who may need you and your family to be his special friend through uncertain times. Talk privately with your own teenagers about proper motives and techniques for helping and befriending the teenager.

WINTER

Winter memories—they remain long after the Christmas tree turns brown, the wrapping paper and bows find their destiny in a garbage truck, and any snow melts into a muddy puddle.

Winter can be a powerful backdrop for family memories because so much that happens in winter involves family. Almost as soon as the calendar announces winter's official arrival, families gather to celebrate Christmas. In many households, this is the most poignant family time of the year and, in some cases, the most painful. With the dawning of the new year, after everyone is shopped out, plumped out, partied and special-programmed out, people usually stay closer to home. They yearn for a routine after a month of celebration. Plus, winter weather often keeps family members on a short leash. Children don't play outside as often. Family outings—particularly to outdoor events—are less frequent.

In many parts of the country, winter is sitting-around-the-fireplace time. Unfortunately, in many households, it's a time to vegetate in front of the TV for lack of outdoor opportunities or creatively planned alternatives. What caring Christian parent wants his or her children to grow up saying that what they remember most from childhood was sitting in front of the TV each evening?

It doesn't have to be that way. Winter offers the time to plan some creative answers to that age-old question, "What's there to do?" Would you like this next year to be different for you and your family? Would you like to make a difference in the lives of people with special needs who need to know who Jesus is and what He has done for them?

Plan to do things as a family to become aware of your world and touch your world for Jesus. Keep it up throughout the year as you make deposits into a family memory account that will yield eternal dividends.

"But when you give to the needy, do not let your left hand know what your right hand is doing, so that your giving may be in secret. Then your Father, who sees what is done in secret, will reward you."

(Matt. 6:3 NIV)

WINTER RESCUE ALERT

In cities and towns of all sizes there is an increased need for assistance for persons who need emergency shelter during winter months. During peak times of need, many shelters overflow with families with children and single persons, all with common basic needs. Programs which help with the additional shelter are known by various names, such as "Room in the Inn." Many of the programs are publicized in the local newspapers. Your nearest rescue mission likely will have a list of specific items they need to supply the demands of the season. Winter wraps, caps, blankets, socks, undergarments, and gloves are the usual requests that many rescue missions make.

Find out what your church is doing this winter on an ongoing basis to give assistance to rescue missions and shelters. Lead your family to join in the effort, providing whatever you can to provide comfort to persons who may suffer or die if the community does not come to their aid.

If you have an option, give your assistance to a rescue mission or shelter which seeks to meet spiritual needs as well as basic needs. Become acquainted with the leaders of the mission and offer encouragement as they perform a much needed ministry.

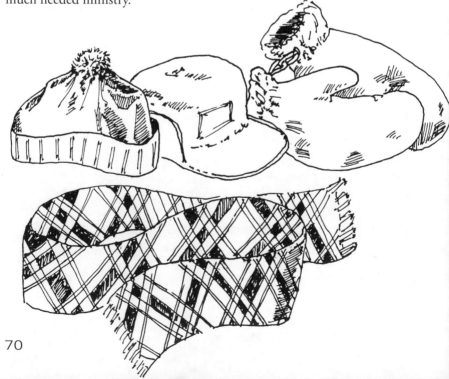

SEASONAL DECOR WITH MISSIONS MEANING

Some churches have special missions emphases during the winter, especially in connection with Christmas missions offerings. This year you can create more interest in the missions emphasis by decorating an area in your home with a missions theme.

From missions periodicals or a missionary prayer calendar, get names of missionaries who have birthdays during the winter months. Select at least one missionary's name for each day you expect to continue this activity.

Assist your children in cutting from green art paper miniature wreaths and writing a missionary's name on each wreath. In small lettering, include the missionary's date of birth below his name.

Decide whether to use a world globe or a wall map with the activity. Place the name wreaths on the globe or map as near as possible to the place where each missionary works. Use small loops of tape or  sticky plastic to attach the wreaths so that the surface of the globe or map will not be damaged.

Begin using the display as a missions prayer guide for the family at a specific time each day during the weeks or days you will use this device to create missions awareness. Each day allow a child to remove a wreath and read the name of the missionary who has a birthday on that day.

As the activity continues day after day, the family may want to discuss theirparticipation in the missions offering the church is sponsoring.

TAPE A GREETING

If you are friends to missionaries who will not be home for the holidays, you may want to give them a special treat from your family this Christmas. Several weeks before Christmas you can plan to make a cassette tape recording of special messages from your family. You may plan with the family what you want to include on the recording. Consider giving personal updates on the main activities each family member has experienced during the year. Let each person who is old enough identify himself on the recording and tell his own bit of news.

Plan for someone in the family to tell about special Christmas activities that will be held at the church during the holidays. Assure the missionaries that you and the family will pray for the peace of Christmas on their behalf.

If possible, include on the recording a special feature of your family singing a favorite Christmas carol such as "Silent Night." Include a brief statement of your family's belief in the real meaning of Christmas. Conclude with the family saying in unison a final greeting or expression of love.

Find out how long it will take for the tape to arrive at its destination. Get a special mailer from the post office so that the tape will not be damaged en route. Be sure adequate postage is applied to the package before you mail it.

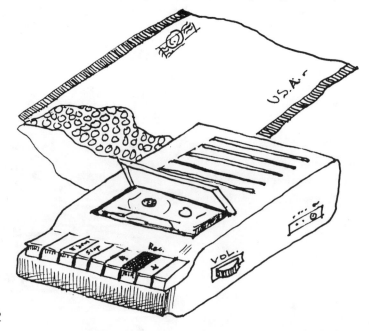

BRIGHTEN CHRISTMAS FOR CHILDREN

Community efforts to brighten the Christmas season for needy children seem to multiply during December. You will see solicitors in the malls, and you will receive requests for help through the mail. Perhaps you will need to be selective in deciding which fund or agencies you will help. If your church or a group of churches in your city are collecting toys and money in a unified way, you may want to join in the effort so that the toys will be presented in connection with a Christian witness of the true meaning of Christmas.

Find out what kinds of toys are needed and whether the toys are supposed to be wrapped or labeled with the size, age, and sex of the potential recipients. Also, find out what kinds of articles are being requested for teenagers. If your shopping days are extremely limited, you may inquire about how to write a check and make your contribution in that manner.

If you discover that your church or a group of churches need help in discovering children to whom the gifts will be given, your help may be needed in the distribution phase. In many cases, church-sponsored projects such as this invite parents to come to a central distribution center and "shop" free of charge for their children. In arrangements such as these, parents are offered Christian counseling, Bibles, and appropriate referrals for additional assistance. Perhaps you and your teenagers and young adults can assist in the distribution and counseling phase, also.

CAROLING FOR THE HOMEBOUND

Various groups in your community and in your church may be planning caroling activities, but your family caroling plan can be different from all the others this season. Consider going to the homes of several homebounds who are not likely to be on the caroling agenda of other groups.

Work with the family to get your carol selections ready and rehearse the carols until you are pleased with the results. Make a list of two or three homebounds who live near your family.

Purchase a mug for each homebound to whom you plan to take your caroling ministry. Into each mug place some pieces of wrapped candy, a package of instant chocolate drink, herbal tea bags, and any other packages of instant hot drink mixes that will fit into the mug.

Set a tentative date for your family caroling outing when everyone can go. Telephone the homebounds and tell them that you and your family are coming by at a specific time to deliver a song and a Christmas wish. Give the person an idea of how long your visit will be before you go to your next stop.

Someone in the family should lead the carols, another should deliver the Christmas wishes, and another should present the mug of hot drink mixes. A teenager or a parent may pray briefly, remembering the special health needs of the homebound, and thanking God for the meaning of the Christmas season.

CHRISTMAS PARTY WITH CHRISTIAN THEME

You can have a memorable party at your home this Christmas with a Journey to Bethlehem theme. Lead the family to think about some ways to carry out your party theme. Invite a family who has children the age of your school-age children to come to your home for a special journey to Bethlehem.

As soon as the guests arrive, ask them to register on a scroll, explaining that Caesar has commanded that all the world be registered. Serve an appetizer and take the guests to another room, exclaiming that there is no room in the inn for any more guests.

Lead the family and guests to sing a Christmas carol, such as "It Came Upon a Midnight Clear." As soon as the carol is finished, a boy and a girl representing Mary and Joseph should knock on an inside door and ask for a room in the inn. Explain that there is no room in the inn, but that they may stay in the stable. Show the children to another room in the house where you have set up a simple manger scene.

After a few moments, lead the group to sing "Hark, the Herald Angels Sing." Lead the guests to the room where the children are waiting at the manger scene. Ask an adult to read from Luke 2:8-20.

Conclude by singing a carol, such as "Away in a Manger." Continue the party with traditional food, music, games, and family activities.

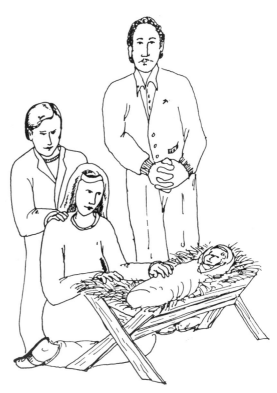

NEW YEAR'S MISSIONS RESOLUTIONS

If you started some missions activities during earlier seasons of the year and have not yet brought them to a conclusion, do so before the end of this year. Then plan to begin with renewed resolve to lead your family to experience activities that will bring about positive missions memories.

Lead the family to join you in making missions resolutions. Lead the family to brainstorm several joint missions ventures you can do in the coming year. Try an alphabetical scheme to guide your brainstorming method. On a sheet of paper list the letters of the alphabet, leaving space beside each letter for the idea the family wants to list as a resolution.

Some of the letters will be easier to work with than others. Fill in as many ideas as possible, then lead the family to select missions priorities to begin working on in January.

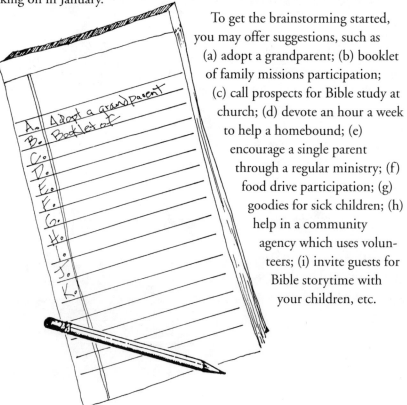

To get the brainstorming started, you may offer suggestions, such as (a) adopt a grandparent; (b) booklet of family missions participation; (c) call prospects for Bible study at church; (d) devote an hour a week to help a homebound; (e) encourage a single parent through a regular ministry; (f) food drive participation; (g) goodies for sick children; (h) help in a community agency which uses volunteers; (i) invite guests for Bible storytime with your children, etc.

CHRISTMAS BAKE OFF

Plan a cookie bake off for your children and a few of their friends. If you have younger children, have a separate bake off for them and their younger friends. By age-grading the bake off you can provide recipes and ingredients which can be more easily worked with and the results will be better. Older children and teenagers may have their own bake off and invite their friends.

Although the desired outcome of the bake off is to produce delicious cookies to give to homebounds or others, it will be wise to plan for the bakers to have a dozen or more cookies to munch along with their other snack foods. Therefore, put some extra ingredients into your shopping cart when you shop.

Talk with your children about the bake off plans. Decide which friends to invite to participate. List the names of the persons to whom cookies will be given. Decide how many cookies will be given to each person and how they will be packaged. Divide up duties, such as covering clean coffee tins with Christmas wrapping paper, writing small gift cards, reading the recipes and setting out the ingredients, measuring, mixing, cutting dough, timing the baking, removing the cookies from the baking sheet, and so forth. Decide on a time to deliver the baked goodies.

HONOR A RETIRED TEACHER

Perhaps you or someone in your family has a favorite teacher who is now retired from teaching in your church or school. Make plans to honor the teacher for the contribution he or she has made to you and to others.

If you want to have an event at your home to honor the former teacher, decide on a theme, such as An Apple for the Teacher, Do You Remember When . . . , or You Did Great, Thanks! If you have the event near one of the winter holidays, you may relate your party theme to the holiday theme. For instance, if you have your event in February, your theme may be We Love You for All that You Did as a Teacher. Carry out the theme in your decorations, invitations, and in the brief remarks you will make during the prayer time before the meal or refreshment time.

If your family and another family wish to cohost the party, you may want to go to a restaurant in which you can use a reserved dining room. You may be able to have a short program of music and a simple "roast" of the honoree. Be sure to express appreciation for the Christian influence the teacher has had during his or her teaching career. You may present appropriate greeting cards as tributes, or you may present a framed message which represents the appreciation of the entire group.

CHRISTMAS GREETINGS TO MISSIONARIES

If you plan to send Christmas cards or personal Christmas letters to missionaries, begin your plans in early November. Decide to whom you will send cards. Consider sending cards to all missionaries whom you know personally. In addition, consider sending cards to missionaries who are natives of your state. You can get current names and addresses from a missionary directory or from the agency through which the missionaries were appointed to their places of service.

Remember that the missionaries in some areas of the world often do not get much mail. Your Christmas greetings can help to encourage the missionaries and remind them that you and your family are among the host of Christians who are in the homeland praying and giving so that they can effectively tell the good news in their places of service.

If you wish to make a distinctive card just from your family, you may want to get multiple copies of a favorite family snapshot and put them into lightweight photo holders. Or you may want to write your greetings in letter form and take it to a printing shop and have multiple copies made.

Purchase Christmas stamps with a Christian theme and post the overseas mail so that it will arrive in time for Christmas. Ask your postal service personnel for advice on when to mail to specific locations.

NEIGHBORHOOD MAP

In many places in the United States residents of towns and cities do not know many of their neighbors. Your family may want to take the initiative in breaking the barrier of silence and becoming acquainted with persons who live near you. Becoming acquainted is a first step in becoming friends to neighbors and in eventually becoming a Christian witness to nonbelievers.

Explain to the children that they can make a neighborhood map which shows each home within an agreed-upon distance from your home. Provide a three-foot strip of art paper or a piece of poster board, rulers, and pencils with erasers. Begin by instructing the children to draw your home in the center of the paper if the majority of homes in your area are almost equal in number on all sides of your home. If most of the homes are to the left or right of your home, the children should draw your home left or right on the paper so that there will be room for the drawings of the other homes. Notice in the illustration that the drawings are like the homes would be seen from the air. Names of family members can be written on the squares and rectangles that represent homes in the area.

Plan to keep the map, using it as your guide in meeting families in your area, beginning this winter and continuing throughout the coming year.

COLD DAY ENTERTAINMENT

On a wintery day when the children cannot play outside for very long, you may provide an entertaining activity with a missions value. Provide materials for the children to use in making Bible verse puzzles to exchange with one another and work.

The puzzles may be made in the form of words arranged in dot-to-dot form, in monk-style writing in which all the words are written with no spaces between words, in jigsaw puzzle form, and in crossword puzzle form. Younger children may choose from some of the simpler methods. Older children may try the more complicated crossword puzzles. The children may choose which version of the Bible to use in preparing their puzzles.

Provide the art materials needed and suggest Bible verses with missions themes, such as: Matthew 28:19-20; John 3:16; John 3:3; John 6:33; John 8:12; and John 11:25. You may choose other verses which are family favorites. Younger children may use Bible thoughts rather than entire verses.

MEAL FOR MISSIONARIES AT HOME ON FURLOUGH

Find out whether there are missionaries spending their furlough in your area. Meet the missionaries and arrange a time for them to have a meal with your family. If the missionaries have children about the ages of your children, you may want to plan part of the menu with the children in mind. Include your children in as many of the preparations as possible. Put the older children in charge of making suggestions about after-the-meal activities that will appeal to each age group represented among family and missionary family guests.

If the date agreed upon is near one of the winter holidays, you may want to use the holiday theme in your meal and in your table setting. You may want to have a salad buffet and prepare a variety of salads which are easy to serve no matter what your serving arrangements are like.

Remember that the main purpose of the get-together is to get better acquainted with the missionaries, let them know that you are interested in them and in the work they do, and give them and your family some pleasant moments to recall in years to come.

PLAN A NATIVITY SCENE

Your family may enjoy building or arranging an outdoor nativity scene as a witness to your belief in the importance of the Christmas message. Explain to the children that in some countries Christians do not have the freedom to celebrate Christmas openly, but that in this country we do have freedom to use an outdoor nativity scene and put up decorations that passers-by can see. Plan to exercise your freedom to witness through your outdoor nativity scene.

If you live in a neighborhood which has front lawns, you may want to put figures of your nativity scene halfway between your house and the street. If you have wood-shop equipment, you may cut out wooden shapes and paint details on the figures. If you wish, the family may put on biblical costumes and pose as a live nativity scene for a few minutes for several evenings, depending on climate and other conditions.

If you cannot have an outdoor scene, arrange a nativity scene on a table inside your home. Use the scene as an opportunity to talk with the children about the details of the Christmas story. If you have non-Christian guests, proudly show them your nativity scene and express your joy that God sent His Son to be the Saviour of the world.

SEND MESSAGES OF LOVE

February is generally known as the season of expressing love for family and friends. Your family may experience love in such an abundance that it is easy to take for granted that everyone has the same blessing. However, there are many people who do not receive enough assurance that they are loved.

Lead your family to send Christian love messages to people who need to be reminded that they are loved. Decide what kinds of greetings you will send. Will it be homemade greeting cards, a fax, a Valentine card which you purchased, or a phone call? You and the family may choose a variety of methods to use in expressing your love to others. Be sure to include on your list persons whom you have not seen for a long time, persons who do not have many surviving friends and family members, and persons who have experienced personal grief and loss during the past year.

After you decide on the content of your message, select the method(s) for delivering your messages. Get up-to-date addresses for each of the persons on your list and mail messages in time to reach the persons a day or two before Valentine's Day. Include the children in getting the mailing ready to send. However, if you choose other methods, include the children as appropriate.

CELEBRATION OF INTERNATIONAL FRIENDS

Plan with your family a celebration of American heritage with several international friends as your guests. During February celebrate the blessings of democracy, using a historical theme such as Presidents' Day.

If the internationals are working on their naturalization studies, they may be familiar with some of the things you represent in the decor of your celebration. The children can help with decisions about decorations and menu.

You may need to have your celebration indoors because of winter weather. If so, keep arrangements simple. If you wish, find out about some favorite foods of early times in the United States. For appetizers make small amounts of some of the foods that you think your guests would like to taste. As the main dish, feature Yankee pot roast and biscuits or another choice which will be warm, colorful, and tasty.

Lead your children to research games that were played in pioneer America and select some games that they can play with the international children.

During the celebration, explain that because of our ancestors' efforts we enjoy many special freedoms, among them freedom of religion. Plan to offer thanks to God for the food, for good friends, and for freedom.

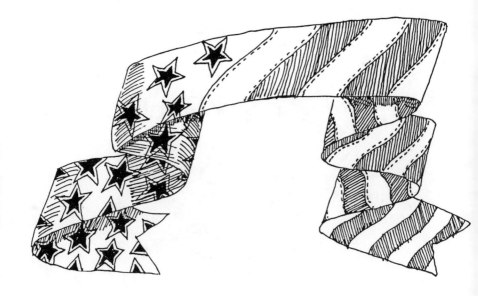

KITE-FLYING EVENT FOR SINGLE GUESTS

If you have established rapport with singles from your neighborhood or from your congregation, plan to invite them to join your family for a kite-flying event. If the singles have kites, ask them to be prepared to bring their kites. Otherwise, buy several inexpensive kites, tails, and string, and let the older children assemble them. Check the long-range weather forecast and invite one, two, or more single friends to join your family for a soup and sandwich lunch before you load up in cars and go to a place known for its kite-flying environment.

Encourage your children to team up with the guests and fly the kites. Devise a contest with recognition for the team who gets their kite up first, the team who keeps the kite up the longest, and so forth. If it is a cold day, kite flyers may enjoy a warm drink from your Thermos jug. Take plenty of disposable cups and a litter bag.

When interest begins to wane, load everyone back into the cars and go back to your house for an informal time of watching videotapes and conversation. Provide light snacks for the group.

During the fellowship time continue to develop friendships with the singles, encouraging them in their individual interests and bonding with them so they will feel more love through your family and your church.

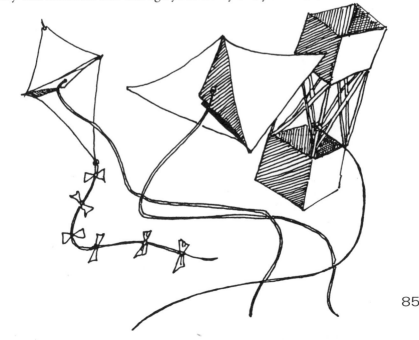

INVITE GUESTS TO ATTEND CHURCH

During a special holiday season this winter, consider inviting guests who do not attend church to accompany you and your family to a special program at your church. Explain to the guests what the program is about. If the event is the adult choir's presentation of Christmas music or the youth department is presenting a drama, explain what the purpose of the program is and explain that the event promises to be entertaining for families. If there will be refreshments or a fellowship time following the special program, be sure that you stay near your guests and introduce them to your friends and church staff.

If there is no planned social event following the program, plan to take the guests to your home for light refreshments or stop by a family-style restaurant and have dessert together before going to your separate homes. If school children need to get home and get to bed as soon as possible, explain that you understand that the fellowship time will be limited this time.

Perhaps a pleasant experience at the evening's event will make it easier for the guests to accept other invitations to attend Sunday School and worship services. Following the fellowship time, express appreciation to the guests for honoring you with their presence.

HONOR PARENTS OF MISSIONARIES

Often the parents of missionaries faithfully hold the ropes of support while their children serve as missionaries in distant places. Many holidays come and go for missionaries' parents without the presence of their loved ones. Plan with your family a way to honor the parents of missionaries during one of the winter holidays.

Plan the entire event around missionaries' parents. Most likely their main interests revolve around the work their children are doing, and it will be fun for them to get to tell someone about their missionary children. If the missionaries' parents have a recent videotaped message from their missionary children, ask them to bring it to your home so that after the meal they can show the tape.

Before the event in your home, become familiar with as many facts as possible about the missionary family, such as names and ages of children, where the missionaries work, and when they were at home on their last furlough. If you have a video camera, make a tape of the get-together, including a greeting and an expression of appreciation to the missionaries' family for their dedication and service. Present the tape to the guests so that they may send it to their children.

DECORATE A CHRISTMAS TREE

This Christmas lead your children to decorate a special tree filled with ornaments that tell the Christmas story. The Christmas tree may be the big tree—the only tree you have, or it may be a smaller tree in another room in your home. The ornaments may be purchased or homemade. The entire family may enjoy making the ornaments. Several styles of ornaments can be used, or one style may be used for a coordinated appearance. For example, all of the ornaments may be made from lightweight poster board and decorated with gold or silver glitter. Or all of the ornaments may be crocheted and starched as stiff as possible. Or all of the ornaments can be made from small pictures cut from last year's Christmas cards. Whatever style you choose, use as many symbols of the Christmas story as possible. Ornaments should include stars, angels, sheep, donkey, Mary, Joseph, the baby Jesus, shepherds, and perhaps the word *noel.*

As the children help make the ornaments, discuss the meaning of each type of ornament. Encourage the children to tell the Christmas story in their own words. Let the children put the ornaments on the Christmas tree. When guests come to your home, be sure that the children explain the meaning of the ornaments on their tree.

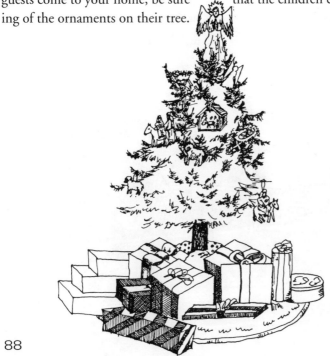

PEACE ON EARTH
BULLETIN BOARD

When the news seems to be filled with everything but news of peace on earth, we need to restore our hope and take a brighter outlook. Lead your children to become good news hounds as they read the newspaper, magazines, and watch television. For several weeks this winter lead the children to make a bulletin board titled Peace on Earth.

The board may be made from a strip of art paper if you do not have a message board large enough to hold an additional display. Place the bulletin board in a traffic area in your home so that everyone can see it daily.

Make a contest out of finding the most news items that tell good things that people have done to bring peace to themselves, to other individuals, and to nations. News articles may include good deeds, rescue attempts, sacrifice, benevolent deeds to the needy, and so forth.

Let each child initial the news item he adds to the display. If the news item was viewed on television rather than read in a publication, the child will need to write a brief report to put on the bulletin board.

As the activity continues, talk with the children about the importance of spreading peace on earth in daily life. Point out that in the Christmas story the angels said that there will be peace on earth among people on whom God's favor rests.

LEARN TO TELL ABOUT JESUS

Children learn about many things by hearing stories. Storytelling has been a meaningful Hebrew tradition since Abraham's day. We can help our present generation of children learn to tell the story of Jesus in story and in song.

Look through a children's hymnal and select two or three songs which tell the story of Jesus as a baby, as a child, and as Saviour. Lead the children to understand the meaning of the hymns and teach them to sing the hymns.

From the Bible, select several verses that capture the meaning of who Jesus is and what He has done. Copy the verses on a wall chart and hang it in the family room or in your children's favorite room. From time to time lead the children to read together the verses that are on the chart.

Although the children may not be old enough to memorize all of the passages, they can begin to verbalize their understanding of the verses by paraphrasing the verses. Through this activity you and your children will be able to tell about Jesus in an informal, understandable, conversational style.

Older children can help you locate the Bible verses to put on the wall chart. They may also write the verses on the chart if you wish.

MINISTER TO NEWLYWEDS

Winter is a popular season for weddings. June is commonly thought of as the month of the bride, but weddings also seem to cluster around the winter holiday seasons. Watch the announcements in your local newspaper and in your church publications for news of weddings, especially those of people in your congregation.

Talk with your family about a way to help the newlyweds get off to a good beginning in their life together. Choose a way to minister to as many of the young couples as possible. Perhaps you will want to subscribe to a Christian magazine in their behalf, present a Bible bearing the date of their wedding, make a wall hanging which contains an old-fashioned blessing, or simply send a card which contains a Christian blessing upon the marriage.

If you are close friends with the couple, you will perhaps want to be the first to invite the couple to your home for a social time after the wedding trip is over and the routine work schedule has been resumed. During the meal or visit, be sure to express your family's pleasure with the marriage and your continued good wishes for the marriage. Continue to be a support to the couple through conversation and by sending greeting cards, and so forth. Be especially thoughtful to young couples who seem to need encouragement from a Christian family.